Shapes Everywhere

Shapes in Sports

Oona Gaarder-Juntti
Consulting Editor, Diane Craig, M.A./Reading Specialist

A Division of ABDO

ABDO
Publishing Company

visit us at www.abdopublishing.com

Published by ABDO Publishing Company, a division of ABDO, P.O. Box 398166, Minneapolis, Minnesota 55439.
Copyright © 2014 by Abdo Consulting Group, Inc. International copyrights reserved in all countries. No part of this book may be reproduced in any form without written permission from the publisher. Super SandCastle™ is a trademark and logo of ABDO Publishing Company.

Printed in the United States of America, North Mankato, Minnesota
062013
012014

 PRINTED ON RECYCLED PAPER

Editor: Liz Salzmann
Content Developer: Nancy Tuminelly
Cover and Interior Design and Production: Oona Gaarder-Juntti, Mighty Media, Inc.
Photo Credits: Ablestock.com, BananaStock, Brand X Pictures, Comstock, Creatas Images, George Doyle & Ciaran Griffin, Hemera Technologies, iStockphoto, Jupiterimages, PhotoObjects.net, Shutterstock, Stockbyte, Thinkstock

Library of Congress Cataloging-in-Publication Data
Gaarder-Juntti, Oona, 1979-
  Shapes in sports / Oona Gaarder-Juntti.
     p. cm. -- (Shapes everywhere)
  ISBN 978-1-61783-415-8
  1. Shapes--Juvenile literature. 2. Sports--Juvenile literature. I. Title.
  QA445.5.G339 2013
  516'.15--dc23
                            2011051115

Super SandCastle™ books are created by a team of professional educators, reading specialists, and content developers around five essential components—phonemic awareness, phonics, vocabulary, text comprehension, and fluency—to assist young readers as they develop reading skills and strategies and increase their general knowledge. All books are written, reviewed, and leveled for guided reading, early reading intervention, and Accelerated Reader® programs for use in shared, guided, and independent reading and writing activities to support a balanced approach to literacy instruction.

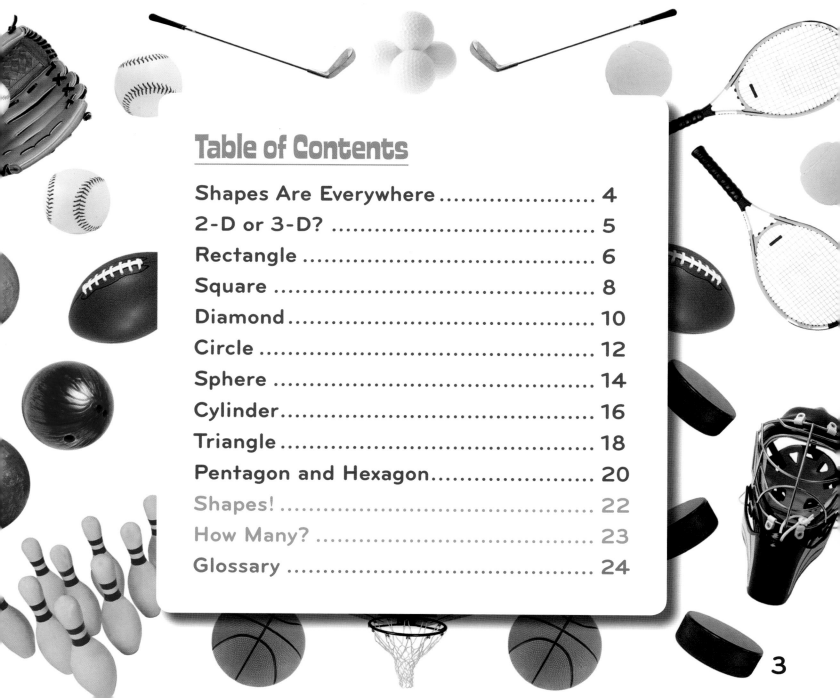

Table of Contents

Shapes Are Everywhere

Shapes are everywhere in sports! Here are some shapes you might see. Let's learn more about shapes.

2-D or 3-D?

2-Dimensional Shapes

Some shapes are two-dimensional, or 2-D. A 2-D shape is flat. You can draw it on a piece of paper.

circle
2-D shape

3-Dimensional Shapes

Some shapes are three-dimensional, or 3-D. A 3-D shape takes up space. You can hold a 3-D shape in your hands.

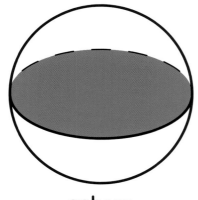

sphere
3-D shape

RECTANGLE

The basketball backboard is a rectangle. After dinner Billy practices shooting baskets. He aims at the backboard. The ball **bounces** off it and through the **hoop**.

SQUARE

The tennis net is made out of many squares. Sara hits the ball. It hits the net and falls to the ground. She loses the point.

9

DIAMOND

A baseball infield is a diamond. The three bases and home plate are the corners. Emma likes to sit behind home plate at baseball games. She has a great view of the infield.

CIRCLE

The **gymnastics** rings are circles. Alex watches his older brother David **compete** on the rings. David has strong arms and shoulders.

13

SPHERE

A bowling ball is a sphere. Alice goes bowling with her family for her birthday. She likes to use a red ball.

CYLINDER

A hockey puck is a cylinder. Josh is at hockey practice. He hits the puck. It slides past the **goalie**. He scores more **goals** than anyone else!

TRIANGLE

The triangle on the track shows the runner where to start. Adam pushes off the **starting blocks**. He is the fastest runner at West High.

PENTAGON AND HEXAGON

Wendy scores the winning **goal**! The soccer ball has pentagons and hexagons on it. Pentagons have five sides. Hexagons have six sides.

pentagon   hexagon

Shapes!

Here are the shapes in this book, plus a few more.
Look for them when you are playing or watching sports!

diamond

rectangle

pentagon

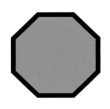
hexagon

octagon

square

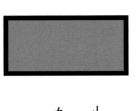
star

heart

oval

triangle

circle

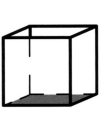
cube

sphere

cylinder

cone

pyramid

How Many?

How many shapes can you find in this picture?

Glossary

bounce – to spring up or back after hitting something.

compete – to take part in a game or contest.

goal – a point scored for getting an object into a specific area during a game.

goalie – the player who guards the goal to keep the other team from scoring.

gymnastics – a sport that involves jumps and other athletic movements and exercises.

hoop – a ring with a net attached to it that is used as a goal in basketball.

starting block – one of the triangular blocks runners press their feet against at the start of a race.